Every Time I Climb a Tree

Every Time I Climb a Tree

BY
David McCord

ILLUSTRATED BY
Marc Simont

Little, Brown and Company
Boston New York London

*The poem "Cocoon" originally appeared in
The New Yorker under the title "Sing Cocoon."*

LIBRARY OF CONGRESS
CATALOG CARD NO. 67-4159

ISBN 0-316-15885-2

PB: 10 9 8 7 6 5 4 3 2

PRINTED IN THE UNITED STATES OF AMERICA

Verses for Young Readers
by David McCord
Illustrated by Henry B. Kane

FAR AND FEW
TAKE SKY
ALL DAY LONG

Illustrated by Marc Simont

EVERY TIME I CLIMB A TREE

CONTENTS

I to You

Not knowing just how old you are,
Whether you live nearby or far,
I'm just as old, young, far, or near
As you may wish to find me here.

EVERY TIME I CLIMB A TREE

Every time I climb a tree
Every time I climb a tree
Every time I climb a tree
I scrape a leg
Or skin a knee
And every time I climb a tree
I find some ants
Or dodge a bee
And get the ants
All over me

And every time I climb a tree
Where have you been?
They say to me
But don't they know that I am free
Every time I climb a tree?
I like it best
To spot a nest
That has an egg
Or maybe three

And then I skin
The other leg
But every time I climb a tree
I see a lot of things to see
Swallows, rooftops and TV
And all the fields and farms there be
Every time I climb a tree
Though climbing may be good for ants
It isn't awfully good for pants
But still it's pretty good for me
Every time I climb a tree

2 THE PICKETY FENCE

The pickety fence
The pickety fence
Give it a lick it's
The pickety fence
Give it a lick it's
A clickety fence
Give it a lick it's
A lickety fence
Give it a lick
Give it a lick
Give it a lick
With a rickety stick
Pickety
Pickety
Pickety
Pick

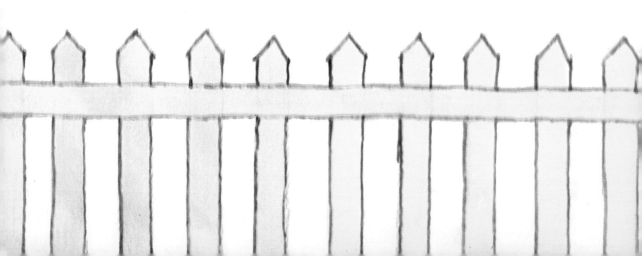

3 SCAT! SCITTEN!

Even though
    a cat has a kitten,
    not a rat has a ritten,
    not a bat has a bitten,
    not a gnat has a gnitten,
    not a sprat has a spritten.
    That is that — that is thitten.

4 GLOWWORM

Never talk down to a glowworm —
Such as *What do you knowworm?*
How's it down belowworm?
Guess you're quite a slowworm.
No. Just say
        Helloworm!

5 COCOON

The little caterpillar creeps
Awhile before in silk it sleeps.
It sleeps awhile before it flies,
And flies awhile before it dies,
And that's the end of three good tries.

6 ISABEL JONES & CURABEL LEE

Isabel Jones & Curabel Lee
Lived on butter and bread and tea,
And as to that they would both agree:
Isabel, Curabel, Jones & Lee.

Isabel said: While prunes have stones
They aren't a promising food for Jones;
Curabel said: Well, as for me,
Tripe is a terrible thing for Lee.

There's not a dish of fowl or fish
For which we wish, said I. & C.
And that is why until we die
We'll eat no pie, nor beg nor buy
But butter and bread and a trace of tea.
(Signed) *Isabel Jones & Curabel Lee.*

7 LOST

I have a little turtle
Name of Myrtle.
I have an extra lizard
Name of Wizard.
I have two kinds of snake:
Bill and Blake.
I have a dandy hutch
Without the rabbit.
If you see any such,
Will you please grab it?

8 FAT FATHER ROBIN

Fat father robin,
A red rubber ball,
Rolls across the lawn
And bounces off the wall.

Rolls, bounces, rolls away,
Hearing in the ground
The worm talking tunnel
And the mole saying mound.

9 JAM

"Spread," said Toast to Butter,
  And Butter spread.
"That's better, Butter,"
  Toast said.

"Jam," said Butter to Toast.
"Where are you, Jam,
  When we need you most?"
Jam: "Here I am,

Strawberry, trickly and sweet.
  How are you, Spoon?"
"I'm helping somebody eat,
  I think, pretty soon."

JUG AND MUG

"Jug, aren't you fond of Mug?"
"Him I could hug," said Jug.
"Mug, aren't you fond of Jug?"
"Him I could almost slug!"
"Humph," said Jug with a shrug.
"When he pours, he goes *Glug!*" said Mug.
"Well, *I* don't spill on the rug," said Jug.
"Smug old Jug," said Mug.
"I'll fill you, Mug," said Jug.
"*Will*, will you, Jug!" said Mug.
"Don't be ugly," said Jug juggly.
"Big lug," said Mug.
  Glug.

11 THE WITCH

If you can hang on to what Joany said,
There's a witch's broom in Aunt Agatha's shed.
When she asked the witch, though, the witch said "No,
That broom won't fly, and it isn't so."
If you don't believe we've a witch round here,
What makes Joan think that brooms are queer?

"If you asked the witch," I asked Joan, "where
Was she standing? Or was she in the air?"
But Joan just said, "I knew where she was."
And does that help? I don't think it does.
Aunt Agatha's shed can be black as pitch;
If the bats fly out of it, why not a witch?

"Did you ever," says Joan, "on Halloween
See the big black cat that is never seen
Excepting then? If the witch has a cat . . ."
Well, what do you think you make of that?
And there's *something* funny about the broom:
Who owns it? I mean, it belongs to whom?

12 AUGUST 28

A flock of swallows have gone flying south;
The bluejay carries acorns in his mouth.
I don't know where he carries them or why.
I'm never sure I like the bluejay's cry,
But still I like his blue shape in the sky.

13 PAD AND PENCIL

I drew a rabbit. John erased him
and not the dog I said had chased him.

I drew a bear on another page,
but John said, "Put him in a cage."

I drew some mice. John drew the cat
with nasty claws. The mice saw that.

I got them off the page real fast:
the things I draw don't *ever* last.

We drew a bird with one big wing:
he couldn't fly worth anything,

but sat there crumpled on a limb.
John's pencil did a job on *him*.

Three bats were next. I made them fly.
John smudged one out against the sky

above an owl he said could hoot.
He helped me with my wolf. The brute

had lots too long a tail, but we
concealed it all behind a tree.

By then I couldn't think of much
except to draw a rabbit hutch;

but since we had no rabbit now
I drew what must have been a cow,

with curvy horns stuck through the slats —
they both looked something like the bats.

And feeling sad about the bear
inside his cage, I saw just where

I'd draw the door to let him out.
And that's just all of it, about.

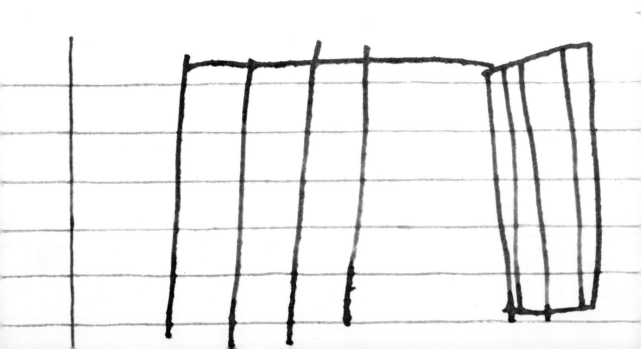

14   THE WIND

Wind in the garden,
Wind on the hill,
Wind I-am-blowing,
Never be still.

Wind I-am-blowing,
I love you the best:
Out of the morning,
Into the west.

Out of the morning,
Washed in the blue,
Wind I-am-blowing,
Where are you?

15 TABLE

Table, I've got my eye on you,
Hoping there may be pie on you.
And if there isn't, fie on you!
Right now there's a fly on you.

JUST BECAUSE...

Kittens have paws they don't have pawses,
Lions have maws they don't have mawses,
Tigers have jaws they don't have jawses,
And crows have caws they don't have cawses.

I make one pause, I make two pauses:

Nine jackdaws aren't nine jackdawses,
Seven seesaws aren't seven seesawses,
Five oh pshaws aren't five oh pshawses,
Three heehaws aren't three heehawses.

Do you give two straws? Do you give two strawses?

17 THIS IS MY ROCK

This is my rock,
And here I run
To steal the secret of the sun;

This is my rock,
And here come I
Before the night has swept the sky;

This is my rock,
This is the place
I meet the evening face to face.

18 FAR AWAY

How far, today,
Is far away?
It's farther now than I can say,
It's farther now than you can say,
It's farther now than who can say,
It's very *very* far away:
You'd better better better play,
You'd better stay and play today.
Okay . . . okay . . . okay.

THE GRASSHOPPER

Down
a
deep
well
a
grasshopper
fell.

By kicking about
He thought to get out.
    He might have known better,
    For that got him wetter.
To kick round and round
Is the way to get drowned,
    And drowning is what
    I should tell you he got.

But
the
well
had
a
rope
that
dangled
some
hope.

And sure as molasses
On one of his passes
     He found the rope handy
     And up he went, *and he*

it
up
and
it
up
and
it
up
and
it
up
went

And hopped away proper
As any grasshopper.

20 BANANAS
AND CREAM

Bananas and cream,
Bananas and cream:
All we could say was
Bananas and cream.

We couldn't say fruit,
We wouldn't say cow,
We didn't say sugar —
We don't say it now.

Bananas and cream,
Bananas and cream,
All we could shout was
Bananas and cream.

We didn't say why,
We didn't say how;
We forgot it was fruit,
We forgot the old cow;
We *never* said sugar,
We only said *WOW!*

Bananas and cream,
Bananas and cream;
All that we want is
Bananas and cream!

We didn't say dish,
We didn't say spoon;
We said not tomorrow,
But NOW and HOW SOON

Bananas and cream,
Bananas and cream?
We yelled for bananas,
Bananas and scream!

21 SNOWMAN

My little snowman has a mouth,
So he is always smiling south.
My little snowman has a nose;
I couldn't seem to give him toes,
I couldn't seem to make his ears.
He shed a lot of frozen tears
Before I gave him any eyes —
But they are big ones for his size.

THE FROST PANE

What's the good of breathing
On the window
Pane
In summer?
You can't make a frost
On the window pane
In summer.
You can't write a
Nalphabet,
You can't draw a
Nelephant;
You can't make a smudge
With your nose
In summer.

Lots of good, breathing
On the window
Pane
In winter.
You can make a frost
On the window pane
In winter.
A white frost, a light frost,
A thick frost, a quick frost,
A write-me-out-a-picture-frost
Across the pane
In winter.

I WANT YOU TO MEET...

. . . Meet Ladybug,
her little sister Sadiebug,
her mother, Mrs. Gradybug,
her aunt, that nice oldmaidybug,
and Baby — she's a fraidybug.

24 JOE

We feed the birds in winter,
And outside in the snow
We have a tray of many seeds
For many birds of many breeds
And one gray squirrel named Joe.
     But Joe comes early,
     Joe comes late,
     And all the birds
     Must stand and wait.
And waiting there for Joe to go
Is pretty cold work in the snow.

25 COME CHRISTMAS

You see this Christmas tree all silver gold?
It stood out many winters in the cold,

with tinsel sometimes made of crystal ice,
say once a winter morning — maybe twice.

More often it was trimmed by fallen snow
so heavy that the branches bent, with no

one anywhere to see how wondrous is
the hand of God in that white world of his.

And if you think it lonely through the night
when Christmas trees in houses take the light,

remember how his hand put up one star
in this same sky so long ago afar.

All stars are hung so every Christmas tree
has one above it. Let's go out and see.